Here to Help

LIFEBOAT CREW MEMBER

Rachel Blount

Photography by Bobby Humphrey

W
FRANKLIN WATTS
LONDON • SYDNEY

Franklin Watts
Published in paperback in Great Britain in 2019 by The Watts Publishing Group

Credits
Series Editors: Rachel Blount and Paul Humphrey
Series Designer: D. R. ink
Photographer: Bobby Humphrey
Produced for Franklin Watts by Discovery Books Ltd.

Photo credits: Bigstock Photo: p11 (Zugwang Images); RNLI: p5 top (Dun Laoghaire), p5 bottom (Nicholas Leach), p8 top (Nathan Williams), p9 bottom (Chris Jameson), p21 top (David Lawrence), p21 bottom (Ray Steadman).

ISBN: 978 1 4451 4023 0

Printed in China

Franklin Watts
An imprint of
Hachette Children's Group
Part of The Watts Publishing Group
Carmelite House
50 Victoria Embankment
London EC4Y 0DZ

An Hachette UK Company
www.hachette.co.uk

www.franklinwatts.co.uk

The publisher and packager would like to thank the RNLI, David Ridout, Glyn Hayes and all of the crew and staff at Weston-super-Mare RNLI.

Contents

Words in **bold** are in the glossary on page 24.

4

I am a lifeboat crew member

I **volunteer** to help rescue people who are in trouble in or near the sea.

It can be a dangerous job.

Hello, my name is David.

What number should you ring if you need emergency help? **?**

When someone is in trouble in or near the sea, they may need help from the **coastguard** emergency service. The coastguard rings the **RNLI** lifeboat station that is closest to the emergency.

A lifeboat is launched and races to help. RNLI volunteers put their own lives in danger to help save others at sea.

My kit

Helmet

Life jacket

Straps

Drysuit

When I go out on the lifeboat I wear clothes that keep me safe, warm and dry.

My life jacket is red. It helps me to float if I have to get into the water. It is secured with straps at the back and front.

I wear an all-in-one suit called a **woolly bear**. On top of this I wear a **drysuit** with built-in rubber boots. When I have all of my kit on it is quite heavy, especially if I have to swim.

This is some of the equipment I need as a lifeboat **crew** member.

Pager – My pager bleeps with a message when I'm needed on the lifeboat. I have to get to the lifeboat station as quickly as I can.

Helmet – I wear a white helmet when I am on the boat. We rescue people from dangerous places, such as cliffs and caves, so I need to protect my head.

Float

Portable radio – Every crew member has a portable radio on the boat. This helps them to talk with the coastguard and **shore crew**.

?

Why is there a float attached to the portable radio?

Lifeboats

There are **inshore lifeboats** and **all-weather lifeboats**. This is an all-weather lifeboat.

The Atlantic 75 is an inshore lifeboat. It can be used in rough weather, near rocks and even in caves. If this boat **capsizes** in an emergency, it can be turned upright again with a special **airbag**.

This is the D Class inshore lifeboat. It is smaller than the Atlantic 75 and is used for rescues close to the shore. If we are racing to a rescue it can be very bumpy, so I have to hold on tight!

Hovercraft are used to rescue people who are stuck on **mudflats** or sand where lifeboats and land rescue vehicles can't reach them.

?

Why do the RNLI use big and small lifeboats?

Meet the crew

All of the crew are on call 24 hours a day. This means we can be called to help at any time of the day or night. Here are some of the people that I volunteer with.

Paul is a volunteer crew member.

Nigel is in charge of the crew when we are at sea.

Brian is in charge of **authorising** the lifeboats to launch.

Lester is in charge of driving the tractors and launching the lifeboats.

Simon is a member of the shore crew. He helps to launch the lifeboats. He washes and **restocks** them after launches.

Glyn helps out at the lifeboat station. He also lets the **public** know about any launches or special events.

Every time a lifeboat is launched each crew member risks their life to help rescue others. During some rescues we need the help of a rescue helicopter, too.

?

How many rescues do you think the RNLI attend each year?

Emergency!

My pager goes off. I leave work and rush to the lifeboat station.

I get into my kit as quickly as I can.

What are *tides* and why can they be dangerous?

?

Brian tells me that someone has been trapped by the tide on the rocks.

When everyone is ready, Lester drives the tractor that takes the lifeboat down the **slipway** and into the water.

Nigel is in charge of the rescue. We speed off.

To the rescue!

Nigel steers the boat towards the rocks. A man is stuck on the rocks after he climbed over the harbour wall. He couldn't climb back up and the water is too cold to swim to shore.

You're OK now.

When the boat is close enough I help the man on board. His name is Jake. I carry out some first aid checks to see if he is OK.

I put a life jacket on Jake and fasten it up so that he is safe for the trip back to shore. Paul radios back to the coastguard to let them know the man is safe and on board the lifeboat.

Thank you.

Why is climbing over a harbour wall a dangerous thing to do?

Help!

Later that day we get another emergency call. A man called Tom has fallen off his **paddleboard** in deep water. He has **cramp** and needs help.

Help!

As we get closer, Andy grabs Tom's paddleboard and pulls Tom towards the boat.

I lean over and pull Tom out of the cold water.

Hold on, we'll get you out now.

Tom has a wetsuit on, but he is still very cold as he has been in the water for a while. I wrap a **thermal** blanket around him to keep him warm and we carry out some first aid checks.

?

Why is it important to keep someone warm when they have been in the water for a long time?

After a launch

After each rescue we bring the lifeboats back ashore. Lester uses the tractor to pull them back to the station.

There are a few jobs to do before we can go back to work. The shore crew hose down the crew and lifeboats to get rid of the salty seawater.

Why do the shore crew have to wash the salty water off the boat and crew?

I refuel the boat and replace any equipment that has been used.

Brian fills in the paperwork about the launches we have been on today. This means the RNLI and the coastguard can see what happened and how we responded.

The lifeboats are ready.

Brian also rings the coastguard to let them know that the boats are ready for the next emergencies.

Training & other rescues

I train with the rest of the crew twice a week. We practise how to launch the boat, first aid skills and what we might need to do in different types of emergencies. Today, we are practising how to use the stretcher on a young child.

Don't worry.

Sometimes we have to rescue animals from the water.

We carry out cliff rescues, too.

Animal rescue

Have you ever seen a rescue? If so, what happened?

Cliff rescue

Helping people

I enjoy volunteering as a lifeboat crew member.

It has been a busy day for the lifeboat crew. I work with a great team and enjoy helping to keep people safe by the sea.

When you grow up...

If you would like to be a lifeboat crew member here are some simple tips and advice.

What kind of person are you?

- You enjoy swimming and are physically fit
- You are focused and don't panic in an emergency
- You enjoy working as part of a team
- You don't mind giving up your time or volunteering to help others
- Most of all, you enjoy helping people.

How do you become a lifeboat crew member?

- You don't have to have any qualifications to become a lifeboat crew member – the RNLI will provide all of the training you need.
- You need to live or work close to a lifeboat station.
- You can volunteer with the RNLI from the age of 17.

Places to visit:

RNLI Historic Lifeboat Collection at Chatham Historic Dockyards
https://rnli.org/

Answers

P4. You should ring 999. If the emergency is in or near the sea you should ask for the coastguard.

P7. The float stops the radio sinking if it falls into the water.

P9. The RNLI use big and small lifeboats for different sea rescues. Bigger boats can be used in more extreme weather and go further out to sea. Smaller boats are able to get closer to rocks and caves.

P11. The RNLI attend around 8,500 rescues every year. They rescue around 24 people every day!

P13. A tide is the rising and falling of the sea, usually twice a day. Tides can be dangerous as water can rise quickly and trap people.

P15. Climbing over a harbour wall is dangerous because you could slip and fall into the sea. It is important to stay safe near the sea.

P17. A person's body temperature can drop very quickly when they are in cold water for even a short amount of time. It is important to get them warm quickly to prevent **hypothermia**.

P18. The shore crew wash the sea water off the boats and crew as the salt in the seawater can damage the boats and equipment.

Were your answers the same as the ones in the book? Don't worry if they were different, sometimes there is more than one right answer. Talk about your answer with other people. Can you explain why you think your answer is right?

Glossary

airbag a bag that fills with air very quickly

all-weather lifeboats large lifeboats that can be used in deep waters

authorising giving permission for something to happen

capsize turn over in the water

coastguard an emergency service that keeps watch on coastal waters to help people or boats in danger

cramp a sudden painful tightening of a muscle

crew a group of people who work on a boat

drysuit an all-in-one waterproof suit worn by lifeboat crew members

hovercraft a craft that can travel on land or water on a cushion of air

hypothermia a dangerous drop in body temperature

inshore lifeboats small inflatable lifeboats that can be used in shallow waters

mudflats a stretch of muddy land left at low tide

paddleboard a surfboard used with a paddle

pager a small radio device that is able to receive messages

public people in a community

restock to replace any equipment that has been used

RNLI stands for the Royal National Lifeboat Institution. The RNLI is a charity that depends on donations from the public to maintain and run their lifeboats and stations

shore crew crew members that stay on land and help with the lifeboats

slipway a slope leading down into the water, used for launching and landing boats

thermal describes a material designed to keep in heat

tide the rising and falling of the sea, usually twice a day

volunteer to give your time and work for an organisation without being paid

woolly bear a warm all-in-one suit worn by lifeboat crew members underneath a drysuit

Index